LORENZO DE' MEDICI
and Renaissance Italy

by Miriam Greenblatt

BENCHMARK BOOKS

MARSHALL CAVENDISH
NEW YORK

ACKNOWLEDGMENT

With thanks to Karl Appuhn, Assistant Professor of History,
University of Oregon, for his careful reading of the manuscript

Benchmark Books
Marshall Cavendish
99 White Plains Road
Tarrytown, New York 10591-9001
www.marshallcavendish.com

Text copyright © 2003 by Miriam Greenblatt
Map copyright © by Marshall Cavendish Corporation
Map by Rodica Prato

Library of Congress Cataloging-in-Publication Data
Greenblatt, Miriam.
Lorenzo de' Medici and Renaissance Italy / by Miriam Greenblatt.
p. cm. — (Rulers and their times)
Summary: Provides an overview of the lives of Lorenzo de' Medici and his subjects in Renaissance Italy and includes
excerpts from poems, laws, and other writings of the time.
Includes bibliographical references and index.
ISBN 0-7614-1490-8
1. Medici, Lorenzo de' 1449–1492—Juvenile literature. 2. Statesmen—Italy—Florence—Biography—Juvenile litera-
ture. 3. Intellectuals—Italy—Florence—Biography—Juvenile literature. 4. Renaissance—Italy—Florence—Juvenile literature. 5. Florence (Italy)—History—1421–1737—Juvenile literature. [1. Medici, Lorenzo de', 1449–1492. 2. Statesmen. 3. Renaissance—Italy—Florence. 4. Florence (Italy)—History—1421–1737. 5. Italy—History—1421–1737.] I.
Title. II. Series.
DG737.9 .G74   2003   945'.5105—dc21   2002001975

Photo research by Linda Sykes Picture Research, Hilton Head SC
Cover: Museo Mediceo, Florence, Italy/Scala/Art Resource NY; page 5: Cappella Medici-Riccardi, Florence, Italy/ Erich
Lessing/Art Resource NY; pages 6–7: Museo degli Argenti/Art Resource NY; page 9: Museo di Firenze com'era, Florence,
Italy/Art Resource NY; page 11: Alinari/Art Resource NY; page 13: Vatican Museums, Vatican State/Scala/Art Resource NY;
page 18: Biblioteca Estense, Modena, Italy/Scala/Art Resource NY; pages 20–21: Uffizi, Florence, Italy/Erich Lessing/Art
Resource NY; pages 26–27, 29: Castle at Issogne, Vall d'Aosta, Italy/ Superstock; page 32: Palazzo della Ragione, Padua,
Italy/Superstock;Page 35: Louvre, Paris, France/Superstock; page 36: Villa Farnesina, Rome, Italy/Erich Lessing/Art
Resource NY; page 39: National Gallery, London/AKG/Superstock; page 42: Scala/Art Resource NY; pages 46, 50, 73: The
Art Archive, London/NY; page 48: Uffizi, Florence, Italy/ Rabatti-Domingie/AKG London; page 53: Christie's,
London/Superstock; page 56: Musee des Beaux-Arts, Marseille, France/Giraudon/Art Resource NY; page 61: Orsi
Battaglini/AKG London; pages 62–63: Muzeum Narodove, Poznan, Poland/Erich Lessing/Art Resource NY; page 67:
Palazzo Vecchio, Florence, Italy/ Scala/Art Resource NY; page 70: Biblioteca Reale, Turin, Italy/AKG London; page 74:
Bargello, Florence, Italy/Scala/Art Resource NY
Printed in Hong Kong
135642

Permission has been granted to use extended quotations from the following copyrighted works:

Lorenzo de' Medici: Selected Poems and Prose, edited by Jon Thiem, The Pennsylvania State University Press, University
     Park, PA, 1991, pages 177, 179–180.
"The Prince" in Machiavelli: The Chief Works and Others, Vol.1, translated by Allan H. Gilbert, 1965, pages 64–65.
The Letters of Pietro Aretino, translated by Thomas Caldecot Chubb, 1967, pages 71–73 and 156–157.
A Treasury of the World's Great Letters, edited by M. Lincoln Schuster, 1968, pages 70–71.
Daily Life in Florence: In the Time of the Medici, translated by A. Lytton Sells, 1961, page 126.
Historia Almi Ferrarieae Gymnasii, as found in Lynn Thorndike, University Records and Life in the Middle Ages, 1944, page
     337.
Girolamo Savonarola's Advent Sermon, translated by Linda Villari, in P. Villari's Life and Times of Girolamo Savonarola,
     1896.

Contents

Il Magnifico

The 1300s through the 1500s were times of great change in Europe. People began thinking about themselves and the world around them in a different way.

During the Middle Ages men and women were usually more concerned with life after death, rather than with the here and now. They tended to accept authority without question. The group was more important than the individual. A life of Christian poverty in a monastery was highly respected.

During the fourteenth, fifteenth, and sixteenth centuries, people began to consider themselves individuals first and group members second. They developed new ways of doing things, such as printing books instead of copying them by hand. People started questioning many of the ideas they were asked to believe. Material wealth became increasingly desirable. And people regarded life on earth as pleasant and worthwhile in itself, not just as a step to the afterlife.

This period of change in Europe is known as the Renaissance. It began in Italy in the 1300s and then spread throughout much of the continent. One of its major figures was Lorenzo de' Medici, ruler of the Italian city-state of Florence. He was known as Lorenzo il Magnifico, or Lorenzo the Magnificent, because he was so many things at the same time. He was a politician, a banker, an athlete, a poet, a scholar, and a patron of the arts. He was an outstanding

Art in Renaissance Italy often combined earthly splendor with religious themes. This detail from a larger painting portrays the young Lorenzo de' Medici as one of the glorious Three Kings on their way to visit the newborn Jesus.

example of a multitalented person, a "Renaissance man."

In this book you will learn about Lorenzo's many accomplishments. You will learn how the Florentines of the 1400s lived and worked, the clothes they wore and the foods they ate, as well as their medical practices and their amusements. You will read about the life of an artist and that of a soldier and about the changes that took place within both professions. Finally you will read some letters, poems, laws, and sermons in which Renaissance Italians themselves tell us about the world around them.

PART ONE

This wall painting from Florence's Pitti Palace shows Lorenzo with a group of architects (*on the left*) and sculptors (*on the right*). Il Magnifico had a passionate interest in all the arts and was famous for the support he gave to artists and writers.

A Renaissance Man

Early Life

Lorenzo de' Medici was born in 1449. He was the older of two grandsons of Cosimo de' Medici, the ruler of Florence. Since Cosimo was a wealthy banker, Lorenzo and his brother, Giuliano, were raised in luxury. They lived in their grandfather's palace, except when they were out in the countryside in one of the Medici family's villas.

Like most rich Florentine males, the two boys received a well-rounded education. They studied Greek and Latin in order to read ancient works on everything from history and astronomy to poetry and philosophy. They were taught how to dance, sing, write music, and play the lute. They became expert at horseback riding and swordsmanship. In the countryside they hunted, often using trained hawks or falcons to help them. They also gardened, bred rabbits and racehorses, and experimented in the production of cheeses. In both city and countryside they learned to appreciate fine paintings, magnificent bronzes, and other works of art. They also received a thorough upbringing in the Catholic faith.

Lorenzo was a charming, friendly, and considerate young man. He loved animals and usually fed his horse himself instead of having a groom do so. He was very strong and energetic, and liked to play practical jokes. He was also extremely competitive. He got very upset if others beat him at a game or surpassed him in some intellectual activity.

Cosimo de' Medici had this villa north of Florence renovated by the famous architect Michelozzo. Lorenzo spent much of his childhood here and often returned to it as an adult.

Lorenzo was tall and dark, but not handsome. He had a heavy jaw, a long flat nose that looked as if it had been broken, bumpy eyebrows, and a high-pitched nasal voice. Yet when he spoke, he was so expressive and animated that "few noticed his defects."

When Lorenzo was fifteen his grandfather died and was succeeded as ruler of Florence by Lorenzo's father, Piero the Gouty. Over the next several years, Piero sent his older son on various diplomatic and financial missions. Lorenzo met with the rulers of other city-states, including the pope in Rome. He also familiarized himself with the actvities of the Rome branch of the Medici bank.

A Strategic Marriage

When Lorenzo turned nineteen, the family decided the time had come for him to marry. His chosen bride was Clarice Orsini, a red-haired, sixteen-year-old Roman heiress. Lorenzo's mother, who went to Rome to inspect her proposed daughter-in-law, found Clarice to be "a good deal above the average" but no comparison to Lorenzo's sisters, who were better looking and much better educated. Still it was to be hoped, she said, that Clarice would develop style and become more intellectual after living in Florence for a few years.

Most Florentines at first disapproved of the proposed marriage. It was customary for the city's rich and influential families to marry among themselves. Why were the Medici looking elsewhere? But Piero felt otherwise. By marrying outside of Florence, Lorenzo would avoid any jealousy on the part of the Florentine families whose marriageable daughters had not been selected. Then too, the Orsini family was very well connected. They owned vast estates and could provide money if needed; they could raise a large army in the event of war; and they had a strong tie to the pope through Clarice's uncle, who was a cardinal. The two families agreed on a dowry, and Lorenzo and Clarice were married in Rome.

To help reconcile Florence's citizens to the marriage, the Medici held a splendid tournament, complete with knights, heralds, trumpeters, fifers, a beautiful "Queen of the Tournament" (who happened to be Lorenzo's mistress), and a competition with lance and sword in which Lorenzo won first prize. When Clarice arrived in Florence four months later, in June 1469, the Medici threw five huge banquets in celebration. The feasting, dances, and theatricals lasted for three days.

The city of Florence lies on both sides of the Arno River in northern Italy. Beyond the city walls can be seen the fields, olive trees, and rolling hills of the countryside.

The Pazzi Conspiracy

A few months after the marriage Piero died, and Lorenzo became ruler of Florence at the age of twenty. He found himself facing a number of problems.

The first was keeping Florence safe from attack. The city-state was threatened on several fronts. There were the other major Italian city-states: Milan, the Kingdom of Naples, Rome, and Venice. Each wanted more power and territory, and each was ready to attack a neighbor that showed any sign of weakness. Then there were France and Spain, both of which were becoming increasingly ambitious about conquering other lands, including parts of Italy. Finally there were the Turks, who were expanding westward and getting ever closer to the Italian peninsula.

The second problem that confronted Lorenzo was Sixtus IV, who became pope in 1471. In those years popes ruled Rome and acted like the rulers of other city-states. They ran elaborate courts and formed military alliances. They also bought cities and gave them to their relatives. Sixtus IV bought a city near Florence's northern border and gave it to a nephew. Lorenzo had wanted to buy the city himself in order to protect Florence's trade route to the Adriatic Sea. The money for the pope's purchase had been lent by the Florentine Pazzi family, whose bank was a rival of the

Medici bank. To reward the Pazzi for the loan, the pope made them his official bankers. In turn, Lorenzo tried to force the Pazzi bank into bankruptcy.

Pope Sixtus IV, enthroned in state, holds court in a magnificently decorated audience chamber.

Matters did not end there. Sixtus IV appointed a member of a family hostile to the Medici to serve as archbishop in Pisa, a city controlled by Florence. Enraged at the pope's act, Lorenzo called out troops to prevent the new archbishop from taking office. Finally the pope's nephew, the archbishop, and the Pazzi family got together and decided that the only thing to do was to kill Lorenzo and his brother and add Florence to the papal territories.

The conspirators chose Easter Sunday, April 26, 1478, as the day for their attempted coup. The place was Florence's cathedral, with its red, eight-sided dome that dominated the city's skyline. Lorenzo was up front near the choir. Giuliano was farther back among the worshipers. At a pause in the service, Francesco de' Pazzi and an associate stabbed Giuliano to death. Lorenzo, realizing what was happening, jumped over the altar rail and fought his way into one of the cathedral's rooms. A friend shut the doors behind him to keep the murderers out. Another friend helped him escape through a back way.

The conspirators had hoped that the people of Florence would rise up in arms against the Medici. Instead the Florentines turned on the conspirators and hanged Francesco de' Pazzi and the archbishop of Pisa from the windows of the city hall. Other conspirators were simply hurled out the windows to smash into the courtyard below. The head of the Pazzi family was seized, tortured, and executed. After he was buried, some boys dug up his corpse and dragged it through the city's streets before tossing it into the river. In all about eighty members of the conspiracy died, while another two hundred were exiled or ruined.

War with the Pope

Sixtus's rage knew no bounds. Not only had the plot against the Medici failed, but an archbishop had been hanged! The pope promptly seized all property in Rome that was owned by Florentines. He also threw the Florentine merchants and bankers working in Rome into jail. Next he excommunicated Lorenzo, "that son of . . . [wickedness] and foster-child of . . . [hell]." Excommunication meant that a person was no longer considered a member of the Church and therefore would automatically go to hell when he or she died. The pope also excommunicated all Florentines. Lastly he declared war.

Since Sixtus IV did not have enough troops of his own, he formed an alliance with the king of Naples, and the two armies invaded Florentine territory. By the end of the following year, 1479, the situation looked desperate for Florence. Much of the countryside lay desolate. Famine and disease were widespread, and the city was running out of money with which to pay its troops. What was Lorenzo to do?

What he did turned out to be a political masterstroke. Alone and unarmed, Lorenzo sailed down the coast of Italy to the court of the king of Naples. There he used all his charm and persuasiveness to convince the king to make peace. He pointed out that a strong pope in control of Florence would prove a dangerous neighbor. Most popes were undependable, Lorenzo argued; they could not be relied on to keep their promises. On the other hand, "Florence saved would be a good ally," especially since the Turks were even then preparing to invade Italy. The French, who had their own ambitions in southern Italy, added their arguments to Lorenzo's. Finally, after three months, Lorenzo was successful. Naples and Florence signed a peace treaty, and Lorenzo returned home a great hero.

Soon after, the Turks did invade Italy. Realizing that the only way to defeat them was for all the Italian city-states to join forces, Sixtus forgave Lorenzo and the Florentines. Florence then contributed fifteen warships to the fight against the Turks. The Turks were defeated at Otranto and withdrew from the Italian peninsula.

Politics and Business

From then on Lorenzo followed a foreign policy designed to keep peace among the city-states. If one state went to war against another, Florence usually stepped in. For example, when Sixtus IV attacked Ferrara, Lorenzo sent troops in to stop the fighting. When Sixtus struck at Venice, Lorenzo brought the two sides together at a peace conference. And so on.

In 1484 Sixtus IV died, and Innocent VIII succeeded to the papal throne. Lorenzo did everything he could to keep Florence and Rome on good terms with each other. He sent the new pope red wine and plump birds for his dinner table. There were presents of fine Florentine cloth. Lorenzo wrote "courteous, flattering letters" to Innocent encouraging him to do what he thought best and incidentally suggesting some specific actions. The relationship between the two men grew even stronger after Lorenzo's daughter Maddalena married one of the pope's nephews.

While Lorenzo was ruling Florence and trying to keep the city-states at peace, he was also busy maintaining the Medici bank. But although an excellent politician, he was a poor businessman. He failed to appoint strong managers for the bank's branches and was forced to close some of them. At one point, in fact, things got so bad that Lorenzo apparently stole government funds for the

A money changer, with an eye on his account book, counts out silver coins for a customer. Money changers were bankers who specialized in exchanging currency—for example, converting foreign currency into local currency, or making change for large-denomination gold coins.

bank's use. Historians point out, however, that he probably stole only as much money as he spent for public activities, such as "entertaining foreign leaders, bribing diplomats, and traveling on state business." Eventually Lorenzo began investing in real estate as an alternative to banking.

Patron of the Arts

Although Lorenzo devoted much of his time to politics and business, his true love remained the arts. Sculptors, painters, writers, and scholars flocked to his court, and under his leadership Florence became the "cultural center of the Western world."

Lorenzo's grandfather Cosimo had opened one of Europe's first public libraries in 1444. Lorenzo continued in his grandfather's footsteps. He spent huge sums of money buying ancient Greek manuscripts. Then he had them translated into Latin or Italian and printed on the printing press, which had come to Florence from Germany in 1471.

Lorenzo set aside a private park that he filled with Greek and Roman statues and portrait busts. He added a school and invited promising young sculptors to attend. The students used the art of the ancient world as models and began creating beautiful, lifelike sculptures of their own.

La Primavera, "Spring," is one of the world's most beloved paintings. Influenced by the study of ancient Greek and Roman literature, it shows a group of gods and goddesses celebrating springtime. On the right are Zephyr, the West Wind, and Chloris, a spirit of green plants. Then comes Flora, the goddess of flowers. At the center of the painting is Venus, goddess of love and beauty, and over her head flies her son, Cupid. He aims an arrow of love at the three dancing Graces. To their left, the god Mercury uses his staff to dispel the last clouds of winter. The artist was Sandro Botticelli, a favorite of Lorenzo de' Medici.

Among the students was a boy named Michelangelo Buonarroti. Lorenzo was so impressed with the lad's talent that he took Michelangelo into his household and encouraged him in his work. Michelangelo lived in the Medici palace for two years. He eventually became one of the greatest sculptors and painters the world has ever known.

Lorenzo spent long hours talking with a group of scholars known as the Platonic Academy, after the ancient Greek philosopher Plato. Academy members were humanists. They believed in the individual and his ability to achieve whatever he set out to do. They emphasized the need for people to think for themselves and not just accept ideas from someone in authority. They argued that everyone was capable of learning, especially classical learning, which helped shape a person's character. And they stressed the importance of searching after truth.

Academy members were creators as well as talkers. Lorenzo himself was an excellent poet. He wrote love poems and religious poems, carnival songs and hunting songs. His finest poems were those in which he described the beautiful Italian countryside and the lives of country people.

The Final Years

In spite of all Lorenzo's accomplishments, the last four years of his life were lonely and difficult. In 1488 both his wife and his mistress died. He had suffered occasional attacks of gout in the past. Now they became increasingly frequent and severe. He visited various hot springs, but although they helped him feel better, the effect wore off after a month or so. His general health also declined. He lost all his energy and spent more and more time lying in bed and reading or talking with friends.

By February 1492 Lorenzo was no longer able to walk or write. His friends took him to the Medici villa at Careggi, where his father and grandfather had died. Lorenzo's physician kept him warm and dry and tried a new remedy, a mixture of ground pearls and precious stones. Needless to say, it did not work. Lorenzo died on April 8 at the age of forty-three.

Within two years invading French armies destroyed Lorenzo's hopes for a strong and peaceful Italy. The Medici were driven from Florence. Although they were restored to power in 1512, they never regained their former glory. Many of the architects, sculptors, and painters who had beautified Florence moved to other city-states and countries. Economic power was shifting from the Mediterranean area to the nations that faced the Atlantic Ocean: England, France, Holland, and Spain.

Nevertheless Lorenzo's legacy lived on. Even outside Italy many

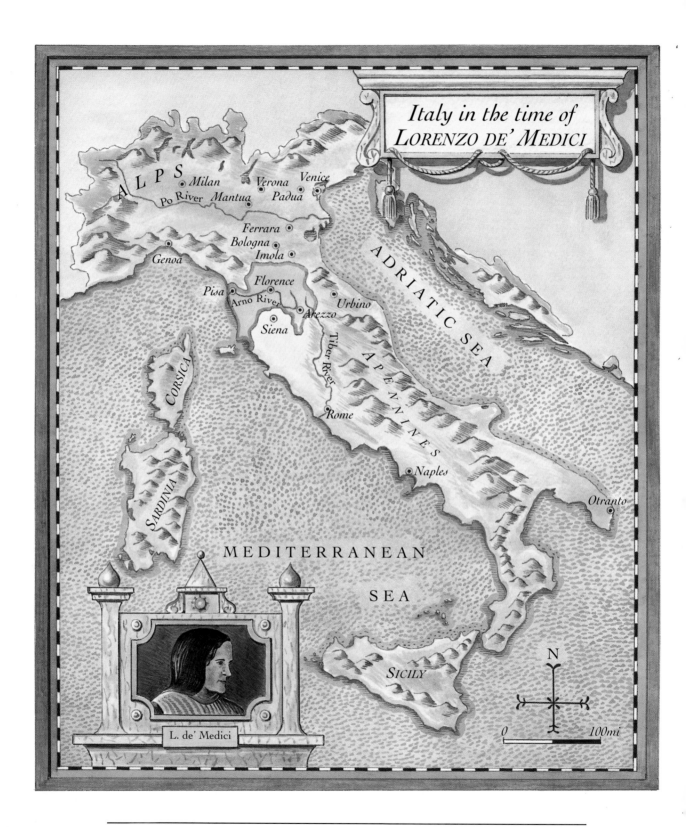

Italy in the time of
LORENZO DE' MEDICI

ALPS

Milan   Verona   Venice
Po River   Mantua   Padua

Ferrara
Bologna
Imola

Genoa

Pisa   Florence
Arno River   Urbino
Arezzo
Siena

Tiber River

Rome

ADRIATIC SEA

APENNINES

CORSICA

SARDINIA

MEDITERRANEAN

SEA

Naples

Otranto

SICILY

L. de' Medici

N

0   100mi

Europeans were imitating Italian manners and dress. They copied Italian styles of architecture and furniture. Like the Italians, they became fascinated by classical writers, philosophers, and poets. Italian artists and tutors were in great demand at foreign courts. As one historian wrote, "Each European city tried to be a second Florence, and each ruler a second Lorenzo de' Medici. Thus the learning of the Italians spread, and gradually all of Europe felt the influence of the Italian Renaissance."

PART TWO

Inside a busy tailor shop, clothes are in several stages of production. One man is sewing, another cutting out a garment piece, which will probably be added to the unfinished garments draped over a rod at the back of the shop. Two others measure out cloth. Tailors were among the many hardworking craftsmen who lived in the towns of Renaissance Italy.

Everyday Life in Renaissance Italy

Merchants and Bankers

The Italian Renaissance was the product of a merchant society. International trade boomed. Vast sums of money moved from place to place. The middle class grew in wealth and political influence.

One reason was geography. Many Italian cities were ports on either the Mediterranean Sea or the Adriatic Sea. Thus they were in an excellent position to receive such luxury goods as spices and silks from Asia and send them on to other parts of Europe. As a result, city-states such as Venice and Genoa became richer than many larger European nations.

Although Florence was not itself a port, it controlled the Mediterranean port of Pisa. That helped Florence become one of Europe's great financial centers. Its money, the gold florin, was honored all over Europe. Its great banking houses financed Europe's businesses and the wars of its rulers. The banks also handled the financial activities of the Catholic Church, including the collection of church revenues.

Almost all of Florence's banks stood close to one another on the same street. In addition they had branches in other cities, both in Italy and elsewhere in Europe.

The banks provided their clients with many services. They exchanged the currencies of different countries. They accepted

The great merchant-bankers of the Renaissance are famous, but most merchants operated on a much smaller scale. In this market, for example, most of the merchants appear to be selling groceries. Notice that two of the women merchants are keeping up their spinning (with distaff and spindle) while they do business.

deposits and kept them safe. Most important of all, they transferred funds from person to person and especially place to place. They did this by means of a document called a bill of exchange. As one historian explains, "Instead of having to carry money along bandit-infested roads or across stormy seas, a man could give his banker the money and tell him to whom it should be paid in another country."

Florentine banks also made loans. Although the Catholic Church opposed the charging of interest, banks had no difficulty getting around the prohibition. For example, a borrower might give a banker a jewel when he repaid the loan. Or an individual might borrow 100 florins, while the banker recorded the loan as being 150 florins.

As you can imagine, interest rates were very high. A popular saying in Florence was that "twenty-five percent interest amounted to nothing, fifty percent would do to pass the time, while one hundred percent might prove interesting." One English king was considered so poor a financial risk that he was asked to pay a rate of 260 percent! But the move backfired. After receiving his loan, the king refused to pay either the principal or the interest—and the two largest banks in Florence went bankrupt.

In addition to the large banks involved in international trade, Florence boasted a number of small banks and pawnshops. The small banks sold goods on the installment plan. The selling price included the interest. The pawnshops made loans on people's tools, clothing, jewelry, and other possessions. You could always tell a pawnshop by the red cloth that dangled at its door.

The Guild System

Florentine workers generally toiled from dawn to dusk. In summertime that meant fifteen hours a day! However, they took a half hour off for dinner (what we call brunch) and one and one-half hours off for supper. They did not take vacations but worked year-round, except on Sundays and religious holidays, which numbered three or four a month.

The typical master craftsman or tradesman owned his tools and worked and sold goods and services in his house. Apprentices who wanted to learn a trade lived in a master's house for anywhere from three to twelve years. During that time, they received room and board but no pay. They did, however, get a lump sum of money at the end of their training period. They were now entitled to call themselves journeymen and to work at their trade. If they wanted to become masters, they had to produce a masterpiece. For example, a journeyman lawyer would compose a lecture on law; a journeyman cobbler would make a special pair of shoes. Then, if their professional or trade organization accepted the masterpiece, they became masters.

Professional and trade organizations were known as guilds. Florence boasted seven major guilds and fourteen minor ones. The leading guild was the Calimala. This was a group of merchants who imported raw cloth from Flanders (present-day Belgium and part of the Netherlands). The cloth had been woven with wool

A stonecutter uses his chisel and mallet to prepare stones for a building. Stone-cutting was a skilled craft that took many years to learn and master.

from long-fleeced English sheep. The Florentines finished the cloth and dyed it scarlet, crimson, golden brown, or blue before exporting it all over Europe. Other major guilds were those of the bankers, wool merchants, silk manufacturers, furriers, lawyers, and doctors and druggists. (Druggists also dealt in spices and precious stones.) The fourteen minor guilds included, among others, the butchers, blacksmiths, shoemakers, carpenters and masons, grocers, innkeepers, leather workers, and, at the very bottom, bakers. Other workers looked down on bakers because it was so easy to become one.

Each guild governed itself and established rules as to how its members should carry on their business. It often set up rules for personal behavior as well, punishing members who quarreled or gossiped. Many guilds required members to know how to read, write, and keep accounts.

Each guild had its own banner. That of the lawyers, for example, was blue with gold stars. That of the wool merchants was red with a white sheep in the center. Members of each guild attended their own church. On the day of their patron saint, they held a great procession through the stone-paved streets of Florence.

Some guilds gave financial assistance to members who fell ill or who became too old to work. When a member died, the guild might help his widow and orphans. Guilds also paid for such city improvements as sewers and paved streets.

Membership in a guild was limited. The children of peasants and laborers, for example, could not join. Neither could women. The sons of masters, on the other hand, received special consideration. If a profession or trade was expanding, more people were admitted into the guild. If economic conditions worsened, membership was closed.

Guild members in Florence numbered about six thousand out of a population of fifty to seventy thousand. Unlike those workers who did not belong to a guild, guild members were full citizens and were eligible to serve in the Signoria, the city's legislative body. Members of the Signoria were chosen by lot, nine at a time, and served a two-month term. During this time they lived together in a palace. They were paid a small salary and also received a beautifully embroidered crimson coat for their services.

The Life of an Artist

Becoming a painter in Italy took years of hard work. You started out as an apprentice to an established painter when you were about ten. You spent part of your time doing the dirty work in the studio. You swept floors, mixed plaster, made and cleaned brushes, and crushed pigments for paints. You prepared wood and canvas surfaces for painting by brushing them with gesso, a mixture of gypsum or plaster of paris, glue, and water. In exchange your master gave you lessons in drawing and using the brush. Sometimes you also learned from older apprentices. After several years you might be allowed to paint part of the background of some large work.

If you apprenticed with a sculptor, you learned how to cast bronze and solder metal. Becoming an architect meant learning how to bake bricks and mix sand and lime as well as how to design a building or a bridge. Many architects studied geometry to help them in making architectural drawings.

After you finished your training, you became a guild member and could set up your own shop. You were much better off, however, if you acquired a wealthy patron—a merchant, a noble, or especially the pope. A patron sometimes provided you and your family with room, board, and money, leaving you free to create works of art.

Italian painters utilized several new techniques. For example, they began using oil paints rather than pigments mixed with

In this portrait, a young sculptor displays his statue of the ancient Greek goddess Aphrodite.

water, vinegar, or egg yolk. Oil paints offer a wider choice of colors. Also, since oil paints dry slowly, it became possible to correct mistakes. Another new technique involved making objects at the front of a picture larger than those at the back. This gives perspective, or a sense of distance, to the painting. The use of light and shade make a painting appear three-dimensional rather than flat. Italian painters also rediscovered the technique of fresco, which involves applying paint to wet plaster. As the plaster dries, the painting becomes part of the wall. Yet another new technique involved applying enamel to terra-cotta, or clay, thus strengthening the clay. Since doing this was also very cheap, even ordinary people could now have some decoration in their homes.

Italian sculptors likewise rediscovered an old technique. They carved figures that stood by themselves. During the Middle Ages,

This wall painting from a villa in Rome uses perspective to make the marble-columned hall look much closer than the city beyond. Perspective was used in ancient Greek and Roman art and was rediscovered by Italian artists in the 1400s.

most sculptures had been carved on the walls of cathedrals and churches.

Italian artists not only used new techniques; they also developed a new attitude toward art. For one thing, they worked more and more as individuals, rather than in groups. They signed their work. They showed Jesus and other religious figures as warm human beings rather than just miracle workers or symbols of authority. They portrayed figures from mythology and history as well as saints. And they painted real landscapes and portraits of middle-class people as well as members of the nobility.

Tilling the Soil

Land was owned by nobles and wealthy merchants but was cultivated by peasants. The peasants formed four groups. At the top were those who had managed to save enough money to buy their own tools and to rent their own farms. Next came the peasants who can be thought of as sharecroppers. They gave the landowners labor and part of the crop in exchange for tools, fertilizer, animal feed, and of course the use of the land. Below the sharecroppers were the free laborers. Since landowners hired them by the day, they were usually out of work for much of the year. At the very bottom were the slaves. These were non-Italians, most of whom were bought at slave markets in the eastern Mediterranean.

Peasant wives usually fed the animals, worked in the vineyard, and often harvested crops. They also took part in the woolen industry. In addition to helping the men shear sheep, they washed and combed the raw wool and spun it into thread.

Soldiers for Hire

Soldiers in Renaissance Italy were mostly mercenaries. That is, they were freelance soldiers who fought for pay alone. It made no difference to them what a war was about. The only thing that mattered was money. If a mercenary was captured, he would often change sides and fight for the enemy of his former employer. The practice of hiring mercenaries tended to prolong wars. Since mercenaries were paid for the time they put in, they were anxious to continue fighting as long as possible.

Surprisingly, battles between mercenary armies were comparatively bloodless. In fact, in most Renaissance warfare, sieges were more common than pitched battles. Italian towns were usually situated on hilltops and were surrounded by thick stone walls. That made a direct attack extremely difficult. Instead an army would camp outside a town wall and wait for the town's inhabitants to run out of water and food. After the town surrendered, the army would move on and besiege another town.

One result of this type of warfare was famine. If a besieging army ran low on food, its soldiers simply stole what they needed from the local peasants. Making matters worse was the fact that the soldiers were accompanied by large numbers of camp followers, including women and children. An army of 40,000 men might easily have 120,000 camp followers. This put an even greater strain on the local peasants, who usually starved to death

Knights armed with lances follow their leader in a full-scale charge against the enemy force. This painting once decorated Lorenzo de' Medici's personal chamber in his palace in Florence.

when they lost their crops and their cattle.

Another result of this type of warfare was disease. Sanitary facilities among a besieging army did not exist, so typhus and dysentery were major problems.

Yet a third result of this type of warfare was blackmail. The commanders of mercenary armies would often threaten to besiege a town or devastate a country estate unless they were bought off. It was common practice to seize a rich man and hold him for ransom.

Soldiers were divided between cavalrymen, or knights, and infantrymen, or foot soldiers. Knights wore heavy plate armor, which weighed perhaps 350 pounds, and fought with swords and lances. Infantrymen wore steel helmets and fought with pikes. A pike was an eighteen-foot-long spear with a steel tip on the end. When massed together in large numbers, infantrymen armed with pikes proved very effective against a cavalry charge.

As the Renaissance continued, new weapons became more common, especially cannons and small firearms. Early cannons often failed to hit their targets and tended to frighten the enemy with their noise rather than kill them. Gradually cannons became more accurate. They were soon put on wheels and pulled by either oxen or horses.

The most popular small firearm was a heavy gun called a matchlock (later known as a musket). It had to be placed on a prop stuck into the ground before it could be fired. A matchlock was awkward to use, but it could hit a target five hundred yards away. By the time the Renaissance was over, armored knights and long pikes alike had disappeared from the battlefield.

Housing

An Italian Renaissance palace often combined the functions of a castle with those of a private house. The ground floor looked almost solid from the outside, while the second and third floors had wide, double-arched windows with shutters inside that were covered with embroidered cloth. You entered the palace through a street door that opened onto a courtyard. Here you found trees, fountains, and statues. Rooms were large and were either carpeted or else paved with marble or colored tiles. Tapestries and paintings covered the walls. Ceilings were often vaulted and painted with glowing frescoes. Silver dishes, Venetian glass, and ceramics stood on display.

Middle-class houses were usually two stories high. The main door was bound with iron locks, bolts, and chains to withstand assault. The door opened into a room that served as a combination kitchen, dining room, and living room. The bedrooms were upstairs. Windows were small and few in number. In winter they were covered inside with solid wooden shutters to keep out the cold. The only light came from the fireplace or from fat-burning lamps. In summer the shutters were left open. Shades of oiled linen prevented flying insects from coming in. Water came from a courtyard well or a public fountain in a nearby square.

Living quarters for the lower class were small and cramped. City dwellers and peasants alike often used the same room for eating and sleeping.

A Florentine palace's dining room features a beautifully ornamented ceiling and walls cleverly painted to make it look as though they are hung with tapestries.

In general, furniture was somewhat sparse. Most people owned only one or two beds, some chests, a bench for sitting, and a table for eating.

Rich people's beds were large and elaborate. They were often twelve feet wide, so that at least four people could sleep in them at the same time. Such beds boasted canopies and curtains that could be let down on all four sides. Sheets were made of linen or silk. Mattresses consisted of cloth bags stuffed with anything from leaves or straw (for poorer people) to goose down (for those who were well off). Poor people, who usually did not own beds, slept on mattresses laid on the floor or on mats.

Chests were a necessity since houses had no closets. A bride usually brought a brightly painted chest with her as part of her dowry when she married.

Rich people usually sat on chairs instead of benches. The chairs had high, straight backs and were elaborately carved. When rich people traveled, they carried their favorite chairs with them.

Cooking was done at an open fire, which also provided heat. The fireplace was tall enough for a person to stand in. As the Renaissance went on, middle-class home owners began replacing the fireplace with an enclosed stove. The stove was more economical. It was also much safer. Unlike a fireplace, a stove did not give off sparks that could set fire to the rush mats covering the floor.

People during the Renaissance took a bath only every few weeks, if then. It was considered "an event rather than routine procedure." The rest of the time they simply washed their hands and faces. Palaces and middle-class houses often contained a large wooden tub for bathing. Two or more people would take a bath at the same time in order to conserve hot water. Other houses provided just a basin and pitcher for washing purposes. Water came from a nearby fountain or well. Although many towns had public baths, respectable people were reluctant to use them. Besides, public baths were believed to spread disease.

Most houses lacked indoor toilets. People used chamber pots instead and then dumped the wastes outdoors. Palaces and monasteries, however, sometimes had what were called privy closets built into their walls.

Food and Drink

Renaissance Italians usually ate only two meals a day: dinner at 10:00 A.M. and supper at 5:00 P.M. Advice on proper table manners included such rules as not putting your feet on the table and not scratching, hiccuping, or cleaning your ears with your fingers during the meal. If you had to spit, you were urged to do it politely. You were not supposed to offer fruit to your neighbor if you had taken a bite out of it. And you were advised to wipe your mouth with the tablecloth after having a drink.

Eating utensils included knives, spoons, slices of bread that served as plates, and metal mugs. Forks were a luxury item, and glass was rare. The basic foods were bread and cooked grain in the form of porridge. Upper-class people ate white bread. Rye and other dark breads were peasant food. Other popular foods included liver sausage and fish that was either fried in oil with rosemary leaves or poached in vinegar. Chickens were served plain, but thrushes were stuffed with bread and sage, while baked geese were filled with garlic and quince. Salad greens and fruits were abundant, but vegetables were scarce, except for onions, carrots, peas, and beets. Among the desserts were figs, pan-fried millet (a grain), almond-milk jellies, and macaroons.

Italians salted their food heavily and generally used honey rather than sugar as a sweetener. Since pure water was almost impossible to get, the chief drink was wine. Most people drank a gallon a day.

Clothing

Men generally wore some variation of the doublet and hose. The doublet resembled a long-sleeved, belted tunic that fell above the knees. The hose were skin-tight and ran from a man's waist down to his feet. Scarlet was a popular color, although patterns of silver and green were also common. Over the doublet and hose came either an ankle-length gown or a cloak that was gathered in at the top and fastened with a clasp at the neck. A hood covered the head. Attached to the hood was a long strip of cloth that was either rolled around the neck or thrown over the right shoulder. In winter the hood was replaced by a fur cap. Younger men often wore velvet caps with a feather in the brim year-round. Almost every man carried a dagger, and often a sword as well.

Women wore low-cut, floor-length dresses with full sleeves. Upper-class women had long trains on their dresses and tottered about on a kind of platform shoe called pattens. The pattens not only made them appear taller but also served to keep dress hems from dragging in the mud and refuse in the streets. Many women wore lace underwear and slept in lace nightgowns.

Rich Italians dressed extravagantly. Their garments were made of velvet and silk brocade embroidered with pearls, gold, and precious stones. In winter they wore damask and furs. As the Renaissance wore on, however, middle- and lower- class people began to imitate the upper class. As a result many communities passed what were known as sumptuary laws, which spelled out in detail what people of different classes could or could not wear. For example, in Florence ordinary women were prohibited from wearing fur. Peasant women in Arezzo were not supposed to use silk except in a bonnet or a hair net. But almost no one paid attention to these laws. The feeling seemed to be that if you could afford it, you wore it!

Two Renaissance gentlemen, dressed expensively and in the height of fashion, stroll through a public square.

Hair and Makeup

Italian men, who had formerly worn their hair shoulder length, now sometimes cut it short. Beards and mustaches became more common, although most men were still clean-shaven.

Wigs for women were very popular. Some were made of real hair from peasant women who let it grow long before cutting it. Other wigs were obviously false and were made from a mixture of white and yellow silk. Blonde hair was highly desirable. Many women spent hours bleaching their hair in the sun and brushing it with oil until it glittered almost like gold. Venetian women often dyed their hair a dark red.

Upper-class women protected their skin from the sun by wearing veils. They tried to improve their complexions by applying lemon juice, vinegar, or a slice of raw veal soaked in milk. They removed excess hair from their faces with tweezers or a paste made from lime, gum arabic, and ant eggs. They covered their cheeks with white paint, reddened their lips with rouge, and washed their teeth with a special formula.

Everyone used perfume. It was essential, for the air was polluted by odors from pigsties, slaughterhouses, and fishmongers' establishments. (There were no refrigerators.) Horses and other livestock dropped their urine and manure in the streets. Housewives dumped their garbage there, too, except in Venice, where the garbage floated through the city's canals. City governments tried

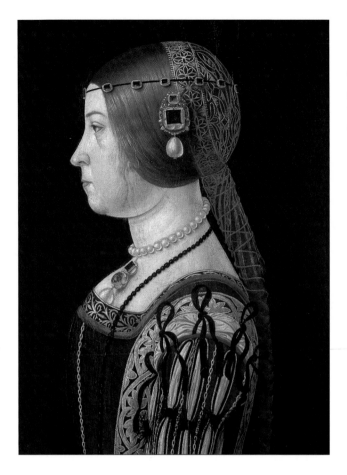

This wealthy woman is adorned with pearls, a variety of jewels, and an elaborate lace hairnet.

to clear the refuse away, but they were never entirely successful. So unpleasant smells remained. People added perfume to their bathwater and carried smelling bottles filled with perfume around with them. They put drops of perfume on their paper money and even rubbed perfume on the mules in ceremonial processions. Witches supposedly used perfume to call up demons and employed a foul-smelling gum called asafetida to send the demons away.

Private Lives

Just before giving birth, a mother went to church for confession. She was warned not to sneeze so as not to harm the child. After the baby was born, she received visits from her friends, who brought fruits and other gifts. The baby was christened in swaddling clothes decorated with medals of the saints. The medals were supposed to protect the infant from being bewitched. It was also important not to cut the infant's nails. Otherwise, people thought, the baby was sure to grow up to become a thief.

Infants were kept outdoors as much as possible. If they cried, they were not usually picked up but were allowed to continue crying. On the other hand, most mothers rocked their babies in their arms, sang songs to them, and played such games as peekaboo with them. The ideal infant was described as being "handsome, fat, merry, laughing and well-satisfied with material pleasures."

Girls married in their teens. The marriage was arranged by either parents or a go-between, but it could not take place until the bride had accumulated a dowry. People seldom married for love. The main purpose of marriage was to improve a family's social or economic position.

When a couple became engaged, the groom gave the bride a ring, after which they exchanged presents. On the wedding day, which was usually a Sunday, friends of the groom stretched a garland of

A young couple becomes engaged under the watchful eye of the bride-to-be's father.

flowers across the street. After the groom broke the garland, the wedding party proceeded to the church for the ceremony. The bride wore a white veil as a symbol of purity. She rode on horseback from her parents' house to the church but went from there to her new home on foot. Two days of feasting and partying followed the ceremony.

Florentines described dying as "entering the great sea." Corpses were dressed simply, in white muslin. Women could not be buried with their jewelry, nor could men be buried with their armor or their flags. The mourners at a funeral wore black and walked around the coffin carrying candles in their hands. Important people were buried in elaborately carved tombs near the parish church. Poor people lay in unmarked graves.

Getting an Education

Many Renaissance Italians valued education. As a Florentine merchant wrote, "There is as much difference between a man with literary culture and a man without it as between a real man and a painting of one." However, education was generally limited to nobles and members of the middle class.

Both boys and girls were educated. Between the ages of seven and eleven, they were either taught at home or attended a public school. They studied reading, writing, arithmetic, and singing. Girls were also taught to embroider and to dance. The typical textbook was a hornbook. This was a piece of parchment that was placed on a board and covered by a thin layer of transparent animal horn for protection. After printing was introduced into Italy from Germany in 1465, printed textbooks began to replace handwritten ones. Public-school teachers kept order by beating anyone who misbehaved.

When pupils turned eleven, they went to grammar school. If they were lucky, they attended one of the new boarding schools that included bright peasant boys as well as the sons and daughters of noble families. One of the first such schools was developed in the 1420s in Mantua by Vittorino da Feltre. Vittorino believed education should be interesting and enjoyable. He introduced

This young gentleman probably attended a grammar school, where he studied Latin, literature, writing, and other subjects.

literature by having students act out stories. He encouraged field trips, taking his students to listen to a political speech or to hear a lawyer argue a case in court. He still taught Latin, grammar, and composition. But he added sports and exercise for good health. He also added manners and moral training. Students were forbidden to lie or swear.

The crowning glory of Italian education was its universities. Almost every major city boasted one. The student body usually numbered fewer than one thousand and included men of thirty as well as boys in their teens. (Women could not attend.) Although rich students at most universities paid tuition, students at the University of Florence attended free of charge. The city government even gave them a small monthly allowance. Medical students received an additional allowance of red wine and spices. This was supposed to "keep up their spirits."

University classes were taught in Latin. The average course lasted between five and seven years for law and medicine, and up to twelve years for theology. Halfway through, a student became a *baccalaureus*, or journeyman. He was considered a master when he had completed the course and passed a public examination before the assembled professors.

University professors earned excellent salaries. They usually taught for four hours in the morning and four hours in the afternoon. If a popular professor moved to a new post, his students often moved, too. If students disliked a professor, they simply dropped his class.

Italian students usually lived in boardinghouses. Each boardinghouse chose one student to act as its rector, or head. The rector was supposed to keep order and settle any disputes that might arise. Students' main disputes were with the townspeople. As one historian explains, "Townspeople resented the students' superior ways, while the students suspected tavern-keepers and merchants of cheating them. Riots between 'town and gown'—the students wore long black gowns—were a feature of university life."

Medical Matters

Medical science made several notable advances during the Renaissance. One improvement was in hospitals. Italian hospitals were very clean for the time. Patients wore white smocks, beds were made up with clean linen, and noble ladies took turns serving as nurses. Florence's hospitals treated invalids free of charge. Its foundling home, the Hospital of the Innocents, cared for hundreds of infants who had been abandoned by their parents because of poverty.

Another improvement lay in the area of setting standards for doctors and druggists. For example, anyone who wanted to practice medicine in Venice had to complete a four-year course in a medical school. Surgeons had to take a refresher course in anatomy every year. Druggists could not charge more than a fixed amount for a prescription. Doctors could not accept money from a druggist in return for sending their patients to him.

Italian medical schools specialized in the study of anatomy. Bodies for dissection usually came from hospitals or from the gallows. Surgeons gradually learned how disease affects the body's organs. Their operating techniques improved, and they invented more efficient instruments with which to do their work.

Despite these improvements, Renaissance Italians employed many remedies that we would consider strange. They rubbed bruises with bacon fat and covered pimples with white lead. Boiled toad was recommended for heart disease, while eating

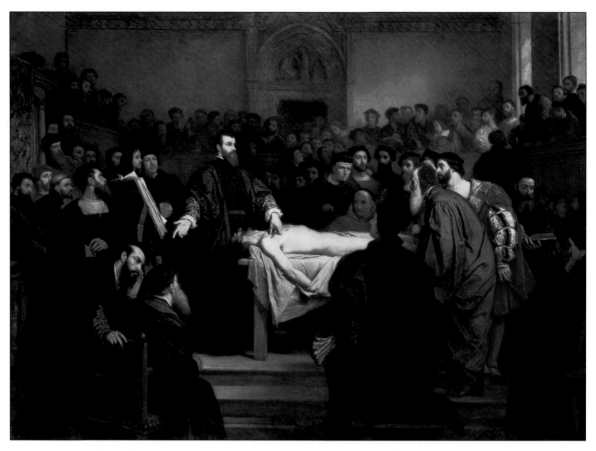

One of Italy's greatest universities was the University of Padua, and one of its most notable professors was Andreas Vesalius. Vesalius began the practice of teaching anatomy by dissecting corpses. Thanks to this and similar innovations, doctors gained more accurate knowledge of the human body than ever before—and the University of Padua became known as the birthplace of modern medicine.

worms was supposed to cure a fever. Sugar was the medicine of choice for lung congestion, and cabbage was regarded as a cure-all.

Of all the health hazards of the time, the most dangerous was plague. There were two kinds, pneumonic and bubonic. In pneumonic plague the lungs become inflamed. In bubonic plague patients develop painful swellings, called buboes, in the armpits and the groin. Both types of plague were highly lethal during the Renaissance. In most cases when plague struck a town or city, it killed between one-quarter and one-half of the population. When someone came down with the plague, they usually died within three days.

Today we know that plague is caused by a bacterium carried by rats and transmitted to humans by fleas. During the Renaissance, however, people had no idea what caused plague. Some attributed it to the devil. Others said it was the result of certain planetary movements. Still others blamed the Jews.

There were only two ways of fighting plague: flight and quarantine. When plague hit a town, everyone who could afford to ran away into the countryside at once. Streets were "empty save for the gangs of grave diggers, silent save for the tinkle of their bells." If one member of a family got sick, the other family members were forbidden to leave the house. As a result, even if they weren't sick, they died of starvation. Infected clothing was burned, and corpses were buried in a mass plague pit as far away from the town as possible.

Some people tried to cure plague by creating movement in the air. They rang bells, shot off firearms, played loud music, and burned lavender and similar herbs. Other people placed spiders, small birds, and containers of milk in rooms before entering them. Still others carried magical amulets with them or swallowed pieces of paper inscribed with a prayer to the Virgin Mary.

Having Fun

Although the use of armored knights in battle gradually decreased during the Renaissance, tournaments between knights remained popular. They were a combination of spectacle and sport. Participants entered the arena as part of a pageant, which might feature a castle on wheels, or enact a fable about love. The tournament itself was rough and dangerous. It had something of the appeal of a professional football game as "half a ton of metal-clad horse and man crashed into another at a combined speed of perhaps 30 miles an hour." After the tournament the spectators, who often numbered in the thousands, enjoyed a banquet.

Even more elaborate than the tournaments were the parades held during carnival season just before Lent. People strewed flowers in the streets and decorated the fronts of their houses with tapestries, banners, or rugs. Triumphal arches went up along the parade route. Floats moved through the streets to the beat of special carnival songs. Dancers and acrobats performed. Many spectators wore costumes and masks.

Other parades were held on religious feast days. There were few spectators, because almost everyone in town took part. The members of each guild marched together. After the guilds came the religious orders. They were followed by floats with scenes from the New Testament and with people dressed as angels and saints. Decorated chariots carrying sacred relics brought up the rear. Such a parade took as long as two hours to pass by.

Many Italian cities held secular as well as religious celebrations. One of the most famous took place in Venice. Boats garlanded with ribbons and flowers were rowed into the city's lagoon. The doge, or ruler of Venice, would stand on the upper deck of the *Bucintoro,* the great state barge, and throw a gold ring into the sea. The ceremony was known as "marrying the city and the sea," and it showed how important the sea was to Venice's trade and wealth. The *Bucintoro* was a spectacle in itself. It was covered with gold leaf that blazed in the sun, while its upper deck had a canopy of crimson velvet and cloth of gold.

The most exciting public sport in Florence was the *palio,* in which horses raced from one end of the city to the other. The event took place on June 24, the feast day of the city's patron, Saint John the Baptist. Three strokes of the bell housed in the town hall gave the signal for the race to begin. The winner received a *palio,* an expensive piece of crimson fabric with fur trim and gold silk fringe. In later years the horses often raced without jockeys. If they swerved from the course into the line of spectators, Florence's government paid for the damage.

Renaissance Italians also enjoyed individual sports. Hunting, either with hawks or hounds, was popular among the nobility. Other popular sports included tennis and an early form of croquet in which players hit a ball with a flat board. Many people went swimming in summer and ice-skating in winter.

Renaissance Italians loved to dance and sing. They danced both indoors and outside. Some dances were slow and stately, while others involved leaping about. Music became more secular. Instruments such as "the rebec, a fiddle; the psaltery, a kind of zither; the pandora, an early guitar, [and] the vielle, a sort of violin" became widespread. Well-bred young ladies learned to play the lute, viol, and clavichord.

Both old and young people played table games. Chess, checkers, and dice were particularly popular. Many Italians gambled heavily at their card games.

Little boys amused themselves by playing with marbles and tops; little girls, by playing with dolls. Both boys and girls made mud pies, sailed toy boats in the water, blew soap bubbles from a pipe, and played tag and an early form of blindman's buff. As they grew older, the boys went in for archery, running, and wrestling.

Italian courts were great entertainment centers. They boasted choir singers, jesters who told amusing stories, pages who recited poetry, and, especially, troupes of actors. Plays were staged both indoors, in the palace hall, and outdoors, in the palace courtyard. The plays were usually comedies and were performed in both Latin and Italian. Between acts audiences enjoyed performances of music and dance.

Noble ladies spent considerable time doing embroidery and reading poetry and romances. They often attended water parties in which they floated downstream in boats, accompanied by musicians.

Many courts had zoos. Animals were usually caged. In Florence, however, they roamed around a court that was protected by high walls. Some zoos contained such animals as lions, tigers, and bears. Other zoos specialized in birds, mostly herons, doves, ostriches, and peacocks. One pope even had a white elephant in his zoo.

Renaissance Italians in general kept many pets. These included crickets, squirrels, rabbits, monkeys, parrots, and, especially, cats

This young Florentine nobleman has a small pet leopard who seems quite content to accompany him on horseback.

and dogs. Nuns in convents could not keep most animals but were allowed to keep cats. Families with large estates often owned hundreds of dogs. Well-to-do merchants kept geese as guards against burglary.

PART THREE

Chess was a favorite game during the Renaissance. This picture of two sisters playing chess, with a younger sister and a servant looking on, was painted by Sofonisba Anguissola, one of Europe's first great women artists.

Renaissance Italians in Their Own Words

With few exceptions, Italians before the Renaissance wrote in Latin. The vernacular, or everyday language, became popular after Lorenzo de' Medici composed his poems in the Tuscan dialect of Italian. The following is one of his dance songs:

Oh lovely women, months I've passed
In hunting for my heart.
My thanks to you, Love, for your part
In finding it at last.

She dances in this dance perhaps,
Who stole my heart away,
And has it still, and ever will,
Up to my dying day.
So kind is she and virtuous,
She'll always have my heart.
My thanks to you, Love, for your part
In finding it at last.

Oh lovely women, here is how
I found my heart again:
After I felt it fly from me
I searched all over, when
I spied two pretty eyes, and there,
In hiding, was my heart.
My thanks to you, Love, for your part
In finding it at last.

Shortly before his death, Lorenzo de' Medici wrote a letter of advice to his son Giovanni, who had been made a cardinal of the Catholic Church at the age of thirteen. Giovanni later became Pope Leo X:

Messer Giovanni, you are much beholden to our Lord God, as we all are for your sake, for besides many benefits and honours our house has received from Him it has pleased Him to bestow on you the highest dignity our family has yet enjoyed. . . . Therefore my first recommendation is that you endeavor to be grateful to our Lord God . . . .

You are the youngest Cardinal, not only of the College, but the youngest that has hitherto been made; it is therefore most necessary that where you have to compete with the others you should be the most eager and the humblest, and avoid making others wait for you. . . . Let your life be regular and reduce your expenses gradually in the future. Jewels and silken stuffs must be used sparingly by one in your position. Rather have a few good antiques and fine books, and well-bred and learned attendants, than many of them. Ask people to your own house oftener than you accept invitations to theirs but do both sparingly. Eat plain food and take much exercise. . . . One rule I recommend to you above all others, and that is to get up early every morning; besides being good for the health one can meditate over and arrange all the business of the following day. . . . Another thing absolutely necessary to one in your station is to reflect. . . in the evening on all you have to do next day, so that an unforeseen event may not come upon you unawares. . . . Keep well.

A different sort of advice was given to Renaissance rulers by Niccolò Machiavelli in *The Prince*. A Florentine civil servant, he wrote the book in 1513, a year after the Medici dismissed him from office. Instead of arguing how a Christian ruler *should* behave, Machiavelli tried to show what a ruler *had* to do in order to survive:

How Princes Should Keep Their Promises (Craft Conquers Truth)

How praiseworthy a prince is who keeps his promises and lives with sincerity and not with trickery, everybody realizes. Nevertheless, experience in our time shows that those princes have done great things who have valued their promises little, and who have understood how to addle the brains of men with trickery; and in the end they have vanquished those who have stood upon their honesty.

The Prince Must Fight as Both Animal and Man

You need to know, then, that there are two ways of fighting: one according to the laws, the other with force. The first is suited to man, the second to the animals; but because the first is often not sufficient, a prince must resort to the second. . . . [A] prince needs to know how to adopt the nature of either animal or man, for one without the other does not secure him permanence.

Since, then, a prince is necessitated to play the animal well, he chooses among the beasts the fox and the lion, because the lion does not protect himself from traps, the fox

Niccolò Machiavelli is best known for his book *The Prince*, but he also wrote a successful play, a history of Florence, numerous essays, and other works.

does not protect himself from the wolves. The prince must be a fox, therefore, to recognize the traps and a lion to frighten the wolves. Those who rely on the lion alone are not perceptive [able to understand]. By no means can a prudent ruler keep his word—and he does not—when to keep it works against himself and when the reasons that made him promise are annulled [canceled]. If all men were good, this maxim would not be good, but because they are bad and do not keep their promises to you, you likewise do not have to keep yours to them.

Pietro Aretino (1492–1556) had a sharp wit and a way with words. So many people paid him not to write about them that he became very rich. In the following letter, he is trying to persuade a friend not to follow certain medical practices of the period:

> *What a sad thing it is to see some poor devil reduced to skin and bones by the diet they [meaning doctors] have prescribed for him when they don't know either the nature of his disease nor the kind of physique he has! That is why his victims first ask for his physics [medicines], then for a word of comfort, then for wax candles, then for the grave.*
>
> *O wise country folk! You do not have access to these pretended cures. You medicine each other, always doing what seems fitting to do.*
>
> *How confident are the Latin phrases of these doctors— and then the patient dies! How often do they hold someone to be as good as gone—and yet that very evening he arises from his bed! That is because they haven't got the faintest comprehension that every single case is different.*

Before air-conditioning, summers in Italy were often uncomfortable, as can be seen by another letter by Pietro Aretino (1492–1556):

> *If knowledge and learning, my son, were as important as living well, I would implore you to go on with your appointed studies. But since living well comes first, I beg you*

instead to hie you hither. For here you need not torment your mind about the devilish subtleties of Aristotle [the Greek philosopher]. Here your one occupation will be to keep yourself sane while the frenzy of this heat wave endures which is so trying to our patience and our poor frames. . . .

As far as I am concerned, I would much rather see the snow falling from the sky than to be scorched by the so-called balmy breezes . . . .

[W]ho can put up with the cruel torturing of fleas, bed-bugs, mosquitoes, and flies? Especially when they are added to the other unpleasantnesses of summer? You lie stark naked upon your pallet [rough bed] and your rogue of a serving man has a good laugh as he hears you fussing and fretting. But he runs off as soon as he thinks you have closed your eyes. You wake up in the midst of the first good sleep you have had. You begin to sweat again. You drink and pant and toss this way and that. You wish that it were possible to flee from yourself and to get out of your own body. So great is the unpleasantness of the suffocating heat that it almost makes you die even as it drenches you.

Indeed, if it were not for your craving for melons . . . which almost overpowers you, and makes you long for the days when they are in season, you would cry a pox on the hot weather just as ragged beggars cry a pox on the cold. . . .

Over and above that, there is better conversation around a roaring fire than there is under the shadow of a handsome beech tree, for under the beech tree you need a thousand . . . tricks to whet your appetite. You must have the song of birds, the murmur of the water, the sighing of the breezes, the freshness of the grass and other such trifles. But you only need four well-seasoned logs to provide all that is necessary for a conversation of four or five hours, with chestnuts on a platter and a jug of wine between your knees.

Yes, we should love winter, for it is the spring of genius.

Not every Italian was pleased by Renaissance society. One Florentine had the following complaint about women's clothes:

A fine thing it is to see girls who normally look respectable decking themselves out in finery, sporting helmet-shaped headgear like society-women, wearing necklaces with strings of little animal-trinkets, and sleeves that are more like sacks! What a stupid, damnable and useless fashion! They cannot raise a glass from the table without soiling their sleeves or when they set it down, the table-cloth. When helping themselves to gravy, they drop more of it on their gloves than could be held in a hood.

Leonardo da Vinci drew this self-portrait toward the end of his life.

One of the greatest geniuses of the Italian Renaissance was Leonardo da Vinci (1452–1519). In addition to painting such magnificent works of art as *The Last Supper,* he studied anatomy, astronomy, botany, geology, and mechanics. He drew up plans for such later-day inventions as the automobile, the helicopter, the machine gun, and the submarine. When he was thirty years old, he left Florence and wrote to Ludovico Sforza, the duke of Milan, applying for a job:

Having, most illustrious lord, seen and considered the experiments of all those who pose as masters in the art of inventing instruments of war, and finding that their inventions differ in no way from those in common use, I am emboldened, without prejudice to anyone, to solicit [ask for] an appointment of acquainting your Excellency with certain of my secrets.

1. I can construct bridges which are very light and strong and very portable, with which to pursue and defeat the enemy; and others more solid, which resist fire or assault, yet are easily removed and placed in position; and I can also burn and destroy those of the enemy. . . .

3. If by reason of the elevation or the strength of its position a place cannot be bombarded, I can demolish every fortress if its foundations have not been set on stone.

4. I can also make a kind of cannon which is light and easy of transport, with which to hurl small stones like hail, and of which the smoke causes great terror to the enemy, so that they suffer heavy loss and confusion. . . .

6. I can make armoured wagons carrying artillery, which shall break through the most . . . [crowded] ranks of the enemy, and so open a safe passage for his infantry. . . .

9. And if the fight should take place upon the sea, I can construct many engines most suitable either for attack or defense and ships which can resist the fire of the heaviest cannon, and powders or weapons.

10. In time of peace, I believe that I can give you as complete satisfaction as anyone else in the construction of buildings both public and private, and in conducting water from one place to another.

I can further execute sculpture in marble, bronze or clay, also in painting I can do as much as anyone else, whoever he may be. . . .

And if any of the aforesaid things should seem to anyone impossible or impracticable, I offer myself as ready to make trial of them in your park or in whatever place shall please your Excellency, to whom I commend myself with all possible humility.

Aldus Manutius (1450–1515), of Venice, was Italy's leading printer. In 1501 he became the first person to use italic type in a book. He specialized in printing Greek and Roman classics, for which he charged as little as possible so that more scholars would have the books available. At times, however, as he explained in a letter written around 1514, he found it difficult to carry on his work:

There are two things especially, not to mention some six hundred others, which interrupt and hinder my zealous studies: first of all, the numerous letters of learned men which are sent to me from all over. If I were to answer them, I would spend all my days and nights writing letters. Then there are those who visit me, some to greet me, some to find out what is new, and others (and this is by far the largest number) for lack of anything else to do—for then they say, "Let's go to see Aldus." They come in droves and sit around idly. . . . I pass over those who come to recite their poetry, or some prose composition they want published by our press. . . .

I have begun at last to protect myself from those who pester and interrupt me. For to those who write to me I either reply not at all, when the letter is not very interesting, or, if it is important, I answer very briefly. Since I do this not from pride or rudeness, but simply so that I may use whatever time I have in publishing good books, I ask that no one should take it too hard, but accept it in the spirit in which I do it. And so that those who come to say "hello," or for any other reason, may not continue to interrupt my work and serious study, I have taken care to warn them, by putting up a notice . . . on the door of my office, to this effect: WHOEVER YOU ARE, ALDUS BEGS YOU ONCE AND FOR ALL TO STATE BRIEFLY WHAT YOU WANT, AND THEN LEAVE QUICKLY.

Florence's first printing press. The invention and spread of the printing press was one of the Renaissance's most important events.

Many Renaissance Italians considered education extremely important, as can be seen from the following decree against ignorant teachers issued by the city of Ferrara in 1443:

> *There exists at this time in this city a seminary of evil learning and ignorance. Our citizens desire to instruct their sons and their adolescents in good letters, and they are sunk in I know not what pit from which they can never extricate themselves. That is, certain barbarous teachers—who, far from knowing, never even saw, any good literature—have invaded our city, opened schools, and professed grammar.*

Citizens ignorant of these men's ignorance entrust their sons to them to be educated. They want them to learn and to graduate learned, but they learn those things which later they must unlearn. Lest this calamity and pest progress further, [the city of Ferrara decrees] that no one take [a] scholar to train, nor hold a school, unless first he shall have demonstrated that he is acquainted with good literature or [has] been approved by the board of the Twelve Wise as suited to open a school. If anyone shall dare to do different, let him be ejected from the city as a pestiferous beast.

A portrait medal of Lorenzo de' Medici. Such medals were a popular form of portable art. People sometimes wore them on a chain or ribbon around their neck.

From 1494 to 1497, the Dominican friar Girolamo Savonarola (1452–1498) led a religious revival in Florence. He was one of a long line of preachers who criticized the Catholic Church and who burned such "vanities" as cosmetics, dice, and indecent songs and pictures. He was also a social reformer who wanted to lift the tax burden from the poor. However, his sermons and actions offended too many people. In 1498 he was found guilty of heresy, hanged, and burned in one of Florence's great squares. The following excerpt is from his most famous sermon, the Advent Sermon, delivered in 1493:

Our church hath many fine outer ceremonies for the solemnization of ecclesiastical [church] rites, grand vestments, and numerous draperies, with gold and silver candlesticks, and so many chalices [cups for communion wine] that it is a majestic sight to behold. There thou seest the great prelates [high-ranking clergymen] with splendid mitres of gold and precious stones on their heads, and silver crosiers in hand; there they stand at the altar, decked with fine copes and stoles of brocade, chanting those beautiful vespers and masses, very slowly, and with so many grand ceremonies, so many organs and choristers, that thou art struck with amazement; and all these priests seem to thee grave and saintly men, thou canst not believe that they may be in error, but deem that all which they say and do should be obeyed even as the Gospel; and thus is our Church conducted. Men feed upon these vanities and rejoice in these pomps, and say that the Church of Christ was never so flourishing whereas our prelates, for the sake of obtaining chalices, will rob the poor of their sole means of support. But dost thou know what I would tell thee? In the primitive Church the chalices were of wood, the prelates of gold; in these days the Church hath chalices of gold and prelates of wood.

Glossary

amulet: Charm.

commend: Mention favorably.

coup: A sudden action.

dissection: The act of cutting apart for study, especially the corpses of people or animals.

dowry: The money or property that a bride brings to a marriage.

fishmonger: Someone who deals in fish.

garland: A wreath.

heresy: A belief rejected by an established religion.

italic: A style of typeface in which the letters slant to the right.

jousting: Fighting on horseback, especially using lances as weapons.

secular: Not sacred or having to do with religion.

solder: Join together with melted metal.

swaddling clothes: A baby's wrappings.

tapestry: A heavy cloth into which pictures or designs have been woven.

zealous: Enthusiastic.

For Further Reading

Brooks, Polly Schoyer, and Nancy Zinser Walworth. *The World Awakes: The Renaissance in Western Europe.* Philadelphia: J. B. Lippincott, 1962.

Bull, George. *The Renaissance.* New York: The John Day Company, 1968.

Corrick, James A. *The Renaissance.* San Diego: Lucent, 1998.

Gail, Marzieh. *Life in the Renaissance.* New York: Random House, 1968.

Howarth, Sarah. *Renaissance People.* Brookfield, CT: Millbrook, 1992.

———. *Renaissance Places.* Brookfield, CT: Millbrook, 1992.

Netzley, Patricia D. *Life During the Renaissance.* San Diego: Lucent, 1998.

Osman, Karen. *The Italian Renaissance.* San Diego: Lucent, 1996.

Schomp, Virginia. *The Italian Renaissance (Cultures of the Past).* New York: Marshall Cavendish, 2003.

ON-LINE INFORMATION*

http://www.learner.org/exhibits/renaissance
    Annenberg/CPB. *Renaissance.*

http://www.mega.it/eng/egui/hogui.htm
    Chiarini, Gloria. *The Florence Art Guide.*

*Websites change from time to time. For additional on-line information, check with the media specialist at your local library.

Bibliography

Atchity, Kenneth J. *The Renaissance Reader.* New York: HarperCollins, 1996.

Brooks, Polly Schoyer, and Nancy Zinser Walworth. *The World Awakes: The Renaissance in Western Europe.* Philadelphia: J. B. Lippincott, 1962.

Chamberlin, E. R. *Everyday Life in Renaissance Times.* New York: G. P. Putnam's Sons, 1965.

Clements, Robert J., and Lorna Levant, eds. *Renaissance Letters.* New York: New York University Press, 1976.

Gail, Marzieh. *Life in the Renaissance.* New York: Random House, 1968.

Gies, Joseph, and Frances Gies. *Merchants and Moneymen: The Commercial Revolution, 1000–1500.* New York: Thomas Y. Crowell, 1972.

Hale, John R. *Renaissance.* New York: Time, 1965.

Hibbert, Christopher. *The House of Medici: Its Rise and Fall.* New York: William Morrow, 1975.

Ketchum, Richard M., ed. *The Horizon Book of the Renaissance.* New York: American Heritage, 1961.

Lucas-Dubreton, J. *Daily Life in Florence in the Time of the Medici.* New York: Macmillan, 1961.

McCay, John P., et al. *A History of Western Society.* Boston: Houghton Mifflin, 1983.

Medici, Lorenzo de'. *Selected Poems and Prose.* Ed. and trans. Jon Thiem. University Park, PA: Pennsylvania State University Press, 1991.

Mee, Charles L. *Lorenzo de' Medici and the Renaissance.* New York: American Heritage, 1969.

Ross, James Bruce, and Mary Martin McLaughlin, eds. *The Portable Renaissance Reader.* New York: Viking, 1968.

Thorndike, Lynn. *University Records and Life in the Middle Ages.* New York: Columbia University Press, 1944.

Weatherly, Edward H., ed. *Renaissance.* New York: Dell, 1962.

Wright, Louis B. *The Renaissance.* Washington, D.C.: National Geographic Society, 1970.

Notes

Part One: A Renaissance Man

Page 9. "few noticed his defects.": Hibbert, *The House of Medici,* p. 113.
Page 10. "a good deal . . .": Hibbert, *The House of Medici,* p. 115.
Page 15. "that son of . . . [wickedness] . . .": Hibbert, *The House of Medici,* p. 115.
Page 16. "Florence saved . . .": Mee, *Lorenzo de' Medici and the Renaissance,* p. 71.
Page 17. "courteous, flattering letters": Hibbert, *The House of Medici,* p. 161.
Page 19. "entertaining foreign leaders . . .": Mee, *Lorenzo de' Medici and the Renaissance,* p. 93.
Page 20. "cultural center . . .": Brooks and Walworth, *The World Awakes,* p. 33.
Page 25. "Each European city . . .": Brooks and Walworth, *The World Awakes,* p. 37.

Part Two: Everyday Life in Renaissance Italy

Page 29. "Instead of having to carry . . .": Gail, *Life in the Renaissance,* p. 89.
Page 30. "twenty-five percent . . .": Gail, *Life in the Renaissance,* p. 91.
Page 43. "an event . . .": Gail, *Life in the Renaissance,* p. 55.
Page 49. "handsome, fat . . .": Lucas-Dubreton, *Daily Life in Florence in the Time of the Medici,* p. 108.
Page 52. There is as much difference . . .": Lucas-Dubreton, *Daily Life in Florence in the Time of the Medici,* p. 191.
Page 54. "to keep up their spirits": Gail, *Life in the Renaissance,* 97.
Page 54. "Townspeople resented . . .": Gail, *Life in the Renaissance,* 99.
Page 57. "empty save for the gangs . . .": Chamberlin, *Everyday Life in Renaissance Times,* p. 130.
Page 58. "half a ton . . .": Chamberlin, *Everyday Life in Renaissance Times,* p. 51.
Page 59. "the rebec . . .": Gail, *Life in the Renaissance,* p. 69.

Part Three : Renaissance Italians in Their Own Words

Page 64. "Oh lovely women . . .": Lorenzo de' Medici, *Selected Poems and Prose,* p. 157.
Page 65. "Messer Giovanni . . .": Lorenzo de' Medici, *Selected Poems and Prose,* pp. 177, 179–180.
Page 66. "How Princes Should Keep Their Promises . . .": Weatherly, *Renaissance,* pp. 92–93.
Page 68. "If knowledge and learning . . .": Clement and Levant, *Renaissance Letters,* pp. 437–438.
Page 70. "A fine thing it is . . .": Lucas-Dubreton, *Daily Life in Florence in the Time of the Medici,* p. 126.
Page 71. "Having, most illustrious lord . . .": Clements and Levant, *Renaissance Letters,* pp. 303–304.
Page 72. "There are two things especially . . .": Ross and McLaughlin, *The Portable Renaissance Reader,* pp. 396–398.
Page 73. "There exists at this time . . .": Thorndike, *University Records and Life in the Middle Ages,* p. 337.
Page 75. "Our Church hath many . . .": Atchity, *The Renaissance Reader,* p. 76.

Index

Page numbers for illustrations are in **boldface**